Copyright ©1982 Foremost Publishers, Inc.
All rights reserved.
This book, or portions thereof, may not be
reproduced in any form without permission of
Foremost Publishers, Inc.
We are grateful to *Antiques Magazine*
for the use of their photographs of *Kingskote*
and *Chateau-sur-Mer*.
Library of Congress Catalog Number: 81-22099
ISBN: 0-940078-01-5
Edited by James B. Patrick.
Designed by Donald G. Paulhus.
Printed in Japan.
Published by Foremost Publishers, Inc.
Little Compton, R.I. 02837.

NEWPORT
MANSIONS
THE GILDED AGE

PHOTOGRAPHY: RICHARD CHEEK
TEXT: THOMAS GANNON
INTRODUCTION: DAVID CHASE

Introduction

"All that has been said of Newport you may safely set down as an understatement."
— James Huneker, *New Cosmopolis*

No matter how often one visits Newport, no matter how much one reads about it, no matter how frequently one conjures up its image in the mind's eye, its presence, its reality, comes as a shock; the ocean setting is too perfect, the amplitude of its Colonial quarter is too great, the magnificence of its summer cottages is not to be believed. And yet, there it all is.

Newport remains the most enthralling city in America. At Newport, American history lives on in the form of an unequalled architectural heritage. At Newport, it is the fortune of beauty not only to delight but to inform — to make vivid, palpable, the story of a nation's progress from colonial status to empire.

For three-and-a-half decades, The Preservation Society of Newport County has led the fight to safeguard Newport's rich and varied legacy of fine buildings. From the first, the Society has not only conserved, it has presented and interpreted Newport and the heritage its buildings bespeak. The following volume introduces the reader to Newport and more particularly to the eight outstanding properties the Society maintains as museums — Hunter House, Kingscote, Green Animals, Chateau-sur-Mer, Marble House, The Breakers, Rosecliff and The Elms. Just reciting these names instantly evokes that special sense of style and luxury that stamps the universal and central impression of Newport.

Newport Mansions: The Gilded Age

Newport was founded in 1639 by a small band of Boston colonists who had left Massachusetts for the wilds of Narragansett Bay, briefly settled on the north end of Aquidneck Island at Portsmouth, then departed Portsmouth in order to settle permanently at the south end of the island where an excellent natural harbor afforded greater opportunity for commercial development. Led by English merchants, the first Newporters laid out their port, began building ships and wharves and entered the nascent coastal trade which linked the colonies of North America and the Caribbean. By the end of the seventeenth century, Newport was a center of British-American commerce and, not incidentally, of privateering and piracy. Few who dine today at Newport's elegant White Horse Tavern are aware that this ancient hostelry was once run by the pirate William Mayes or realize that three centuries ago Captain Kidd supped with his freebooting cohort Thomas Paine across Narragansett Bay at Jamestown.

By the mid-eighteenth century, Newport was at the height of its maritime prosperity. Merchants engaged in various forms of commerce, including smuggling and slavery; the only locally made export of note was the furniture produced by Newport's superb cabinetmakers, the Townsends and Goddards. Merchants built homes along Thames Street and Washington Street overlooking their countinghouses, cargo sheds and wharves. Among the few waterside survivors of these establishments is Hunter House. An ample Colonial mansion, it contains elaborately paneled rooms and a fine collection of Townsend-Goddard furniture.

Colonial Newport, one of Britain's leading American settlements, was unusually cosmopolitan because of its wide-ranging trade connections; because it welcomed Jewish and Quaker traders not accepted elsewhere; and because its healthful, pleasant climate attracted visitors from the Southern and Caribbean colonies anxious to avoid summer heat and pestilence and happy for the opportunity to socialize in a fashion which the isolation of plantation life made impossible. The sophistication of Newport's society and local craftsmanship was matched by that of its resident amateur architect, British-born merchant Peter Harrison, whose Palladian tastes gave form to Touro Synagogue, Redwood Library and the Brick Market. Merchant grandees maintained not only town houses but great country estates. The most famous of these, Captain Godfrey Malbone's brownstone villa, was surrounded by terraced gardens and reflecting pools. Said to be the most magnificent dwelling in America, it caught fire in June, 1766, while the Malbones were giving a dinner. According to legend, Captain Malbone had the table moved to an adjacent building, telling his guests that he would not permit loss of his house to spoil the party. None of Newport's Colonial-era country estates remain intact, but a wonderful nineteenth-century analogue can be found in Green Animals, the Brayton estate renown for its whimsical topiary gardens and gracious, porch-fronted house commanding a vista across sloping lawns to Narragansett Bay.

The Revolution brought an end to Newport's mercantile economy. Never again would this port be a major trading center. Many merchants left because of the war, business dwindled, and building came to a halt. Yet, even in decline, Newport's climate and setting still attracted Southerners, and a growing number of families from New York, Boston and Baltimore. Most visitors boarded at farms and thus there was no center of summer activity until the first hotel went up in the mid-1820s on Catherine Street, just off Bellevue Avenue. The earliest summer houses date to the 1830s and were built on the hill above the port. The best-known early cottage is Kingscote, a Gothic dwelling erected by Georgian planter George Noble Jones. In the very year Kingscote was being planned, 1839, *The Family Magazine* reported that Newport boasted a score of cottages, several excellent hotels and a wonderful new establishment where one could get a hot bath, day or night. Though largely forgotten today, hotels were the focus of the Newport season from 1825 to about 1855. Hordes of guests stayed in these immense wooden caravansaries; gossip columnists employed by half a dozen big-city papers kept tabs on their guest registers and prowled the corridors searching for stories to report on the "lionesses" of fashion.

British novelist Anthony Trollope paid a visit to Newport in 1862 and proclaimed that the city had achieved an international reputation as a prestigious resort. Cottages, not hotels, were by then its special attribute. A boom in cottage construction during the '50s had set this course. A small group of property owners and local boosters set in motion a series of improvements in the '50s which prompted construction of dozens of summer cottages. The central figure in all this was a tailor-turned-real-estate-entrepreneur, Alfred Smith. Smith bought up and subdivided several farms, successfully pushed through construction of Bellevue Avenue and Ocean Drive, handled most real estate sales and rentals. He haunted the hotels, seeking out potential clients. He was likened to a field marshall, his rolled-up map of Newport carried as if it were a baton, riding ceaselessly about town. The new cottages of the '50s were much grander than their truly cottage-like predecessors. The most imposing "cottage" erected in the '50s, Chateau-sur-Mer, is an Italianate stone villa constructed by a New Yorker, China-trade merchant William S. Wetmore. It was the setting for the first of Newport's spectacular parties — a *fête champêtre* Wetmore hosted in 1857 to which he invited 3000 guests.

By the 1860s, it was not fashionable to stay at a Newport hotel for the season: one must own or rent a cottage. Most of the bigger hotels closed while more cottages were being built. There were then 250 summer houses in town: about 100 were rental properties and 150 were generally occupied by their owners. Due to the Civil War, the Southern contingent at Newport was depleted and cottagers hailing from New York and Boston dominated summer society. Writing in 1870, Henry James differentiated between Newport, where "life is public," and the atmosphere of Newport's chief rival, Saratoga, which "is absolutely common." The difference, in James' view, was between a series of "organized homes" and a group of "undiscriminating" hotels. By the '70s, Newport had indisputably become the nation's social capital.

In stating this, however, one must not lose sight of the fact that Newport attracted not only America's financial elite, but many of its most gifted artists and writers, diplomats, politicians and jurists, historians, educators, scientists and engineers, architects and collectors. The literary set, led by Julia Ward Howe, gathered at Newport in the summer. Even that colorful writer of Wild-West tales, Bret Harte, spent time in genteel Newport.

For those disinclined to partake of witty theatricals and bookish conversation, the Newport season was very much a season of sport. Both men and women enjoyed riding, coaching, tennis and croquet. Archery was a women's sport. Fishing, sailing, polo and golf were men's sports. Swimming was enjoyed by both sexes, but generally not together. In the morning, Easton's Beach was taken over by the ladies, some of whom entered the waves in rumbling, horse-drawn bathing carriages. At noon, a red flag went up, the women departed, and the beach was for men only. Those who think of the Victorian era as one of extraordinary prudishness should know that men swam at Newport beach without benefit of bathing attire.

Newport cottages of the 1860s, '70s and early '80s were large, comfortable and oriented to the out-of-doors. In the early '70s, particularly, spectacular architectural eccentricities were erected that have caused "tasteful" critics problems ever since — cottages like architect Richard Morris Hunt's Henry Marquand house, a half-timbered late Gothic pile popularly known as "Bric-a-brac Hall"; and the towering additions Hunt also designed for Chateau-sur-Mer. In 1879, wilful, ill-tempered James Gordon Bennett, Jr. — a yachtsman and rake and the owner of the New York *Herald* who sent Stanley out to find Livingstone in Africa — built the Newport Casino opposite his Bellevue Avenue cottage as a place where people might visit, dine, hear band concerts and play tennis. Bennett built the Casino because he had been ejected from Newport's leading men's club and he wanted to show how quickly society would dance to his tune. The Casino was an instant success and remained a center of cottagers' daytime activities for decades. The work of New York architects McKim, Mead & White, it established a vogue for informal, shingle-clad resort architecture inspired by the contemporary British Queen Anne style and American Colonial buildings. Within five years, however, an entirely different taste took over. Grand new cottages were built, hieratic and palatial in scale, and it was to be the very same McKim, Mead & White, and even more Richard Morris Hunt, who would set the pace in designing princely residences. Their celebrated "cottages" of the late 1880s, '90s and early 1900s make Newport *the* place in America to experience the Gilded Age.

The rush to opulence began with a series of very

large, late Gothic stone houses at Newport. They were quickly overshadowed by a residence designed by Richard Morris Hunt and built by William K. Vanderbilt as an anniversary present for his wife: Marble House, true to its name, is a Neo-Classical pavilion clad in shimmering white marble and decorated with a profusion of richly tinted marble veneers, mantels and ornaments, set off by gold fittings and trim. It is like an enormous, beautifully crafted jewel box, miraculously set down on a cliff by the sea. After the Civil War, a great many American fortunes, like the Vanderbilts', had grown to Medicean proportions, and the proud possessors of these fortunes, familiar with both European society and European standards of domestic magnificence, set out to build on the Medicean model. Aristocracy aside, if the bankers and merchants of the Renaissance (and equally, of the Industrial Revolution in England) housed themselves in palatial city residences and country villas, so too would the bankers and merchants and industrial magnates of the American Renaissance — an era in which this nation was growing and profiting at a prodigious rate and "manifest destiny" and imperial aspirations were abroad in the land. Unabashed splendor was not only accepted, it was celebrated.

Marble House was soon eclipsed by The Breakers, summer home of W.K. Vanderbilt's older brother, Cornelius II. The Breakers, again the work of Hunt, has never been surpassed. From an architectural standpoint, nonetheless, several large later cottages, though less sumptuous, are equally interesting. The best of these are McKim, Mead & White's Rosecliff and Horace Trumbauer's The Elms. Summing up Newport at the turn of the century, a British visitor wrote to the *Evening Mercury* of Liverpool, "No words can convey an idea of the marvelous spectacle of well and graciously and artistically applied wealth which has harnessed to its aspirations the greatest architectural art of the country. . . The result is such a combination of natural and contrived beauty, open for the enjoyment of all, as cannot be seen on such terms anywhere else in the world."

The luxuriousness of Newport social life prompted other observers to write scathing critiques. Yet these same critics were clearly fascinated by Newport, and some did not always conceal the envy which occasionally colored their attacks. One critic who visited Newport during the '90's, the Frenchman Paul Bourget, recounts at length the typical day of a "society lady": She takes a hearty breakfast before departing her villa for a brisk, two-hour ride. After changing, she drives to the Casino to watch a tennis match and then boards her yacht for lunch with friends. Bourget describes the yacht with relish, noting the master stateroom, decorated with old rose damask and white enameled furniture; the drawing room's light-colored walls, bookshelves, piano, plants and watercolors by well-known artists; the mahogany-paneled dining room; a glass-enclosed upper saloon banked with sofas and bright cushions; and the afterdeck set with potted palms, rocking chairs and a great aviary full of exotic birds. (That Bourget begins his tour of the yacht in his hostess's bedroom adds an unintended touch of Gallic spice to the account.) After lunch, Bourget's lady and her guests relax on deck before returning to shore and then going by carriage to a polo match. After polo, the society lady changes again, goes out to dinner and then on to a ball.

The particulars of Newport cottage life changed little between the 1890s and the 1920s. These were the halcyon years of the leisured class. The round of daily events Paul Bourget recounted was described with but few modifications by many other writers right through the '20s. But the tempo and formality changed substantially. The otherworldliness of it all was fading, and to F. Scott Fitzgerald's famous line, "The rich are different from us," Ernest Hemingway would coolly respond, "Yes, they have more money."

Although, in a sense, the Newport scene of popular imagination died with the Great Depression, it lives on to a degree in the much quieter life-style of those who still come for the season, and it is perpetuated in the incomparable legacy of landscape and architecture which survives from the Gilded Age, from the earlier nineteenth century, and from the days of Newport's Colonial prosperity. To see Newport today — to visit the Point, Bellevue Avenue, Ocean Drive and Cliff Walk, to enter Hunter House or The Breakers or one of the other museum houses — is to come face-to-face with a unique and living heritage.

– David Chase

The Breakers

If the Gilded Age was to be summed up by a single house, that house would have to be The Breakers. Measuring 250 feet by 150 feet, containing 70 rooms, the four-story limestone palace is as much a monument to its time as it was a summer home for Cornelius Vanderbilt and his family.

Mr. Vanderbilt at first wanted a two-story villa to replace the original Breakers, which he bought from Pierre Lorillard in 1885 and which burned to the ground in 1892. But the first design by architect Richard Morris Hunt was scrapped for a much larger building modeled after the Renaissance palaces of Turin and Genoa. The resulting structure, covering nearly an acre of the Vanderbilts' 11-acre estate on Ochre Point, was more urban palace than seaside villa.

Exactly how the house came to be so large is uncertain. For Hunt, the imperial scale of The Breakers was the logical conclusion to his Beaux-Arts training and the grand manner he had developed while working on Ochre Point, Marble House, and other Newport mansions. There is evidence, though, that Mr. Vanderbilt had a strong say in the final shape of the house, keeping detailed notes on how it was to be furnished and even pacing off the size of the rooms for Hunt.

As the eldest son of William Henry Vanderbilt, and grandson of Commodore Cornelius Vanderbilt, who started the family fortune, Cornelius Vanderbilt was worth more than $70 million. Nevertheless, he began work as a bank clerk, earning $50 a month and reportedly living on his salary. He continued working long hours, even after becoming chairman of the family's railroad empire, and was said to have been able to estimate his worth to the penny on any given day.

Work on The Breakers began in 1893 and was completed in just over two years, a remarkable feat considering the workmen did not have the benefit of modern tools and machinery. Corps of workers, numbering in the hundreds, took part in the building, laying the walls up stone by stone. Whole rooms were designed and built in the shops of European craftsmen, including Allard and Sons of Paris, then shipped to Newport for reassembly.

For his second home, Mr. Vanderbilt was taking no chances with fire. No wood was used in the construction. The core of the building was stone and brick, with steel beams for structural support. The kitchen was isolated in a ground-floor wing and, as a further precaution, the original heating plant was buried near the caretaker's cottage, several hundred feet from the main house.

For months, as the house went up, Newport society eagerly anticipated the opening of The Breakers. The house, it was rumored, contained tons of art treasures gathered in Italy and France. Taps in the bathrooms reportedly dispensed a choice of pure rainwater or healthful saltwater, both hot or cold. When the housewarming, combined with a coming-out party for 20-year-old Gertrude Vanderbilt, was held on an August evening in 1895, the reality of The Breakers outshone the rumors.

More than 300 guests were escorted into the Great Hall by footmen wearing the distinctive maroon livery of the Vanderbilts. The hall, rising nearly 50 feet and lined with Caen stone, provided — as it still does — a fitting introduction to the sense of space and vista that exists in all the public rooms downstairs. The east wall is almost entirely glass, affording an unbroken

The Breakers, Newport's most imposing mansion, was designed by Richard Morris Hunt for Cornelius Vanderbilt II.

view across the terraces and lawn to the ocean and the distant reef that gave The Breakers its name.

Eight matching sets of doors lead from the entrance hall to rooms of richness unparalleled in Newport. The two-story dining room, larger than some ballrooms, is lined with twelve massive shafts of rose alabaster topped with gilded bronze capitals. The gray and gold paneled music room has gray Ionic pilasters and furnishings and draperies of red Italian cut velvet. The cool grotto-like billiard room is faced from floor to ceiling with matched slabs of gray-green Cippolino marble.

The grand scale was continued behind the scenes in the service areas. Of the 70 rooms in the house, 33 were for the domestic staff. Whether in Newport or New York, Mrs. Vanderbilt reportedly could give a dinner party for 200 without calling in extra help. The two-story kitchen, where family meals were prepared behind sealed doors so that no odors escaped into the living quarters, was large enough to accommodate a normal-sized house. The two-level butler's pantry, where the family silverware was kept in a vault ten feet deep, was stacked with fine porcelain, china and glassware.

While the rooms inside the mansion were no larger than necessary to maintain proportion with the abundance of decoration, the house, seen from the outside, seems to overwhelm its setting. Working with such a huge mass of buff Indiana limestone, Hunt did what he could to diversify the exterior, designing each of the four levels separately. Artistically, critics agree, the east side facing the water is the most successful, primarily because of the arched double loggia that fills the space between the massive end wings. The loggias had a practical purpose as well. During the summer season they were furnished and used as outdoor living rooms.

Despite the success of their housewarming and their great wealth, the Vanderbilts were not particularly noted for their entertaining. Mr. Vanderbilt kept busy with the family business, but still devoted hours each day to philanthropic activities. Besides his time, he donated upwards of a million dollars a year to various charities, much of it anonymously. He was a devout man — he and his wife, the former Alice Claypoole Gwynne, had met while teaching Sunday school — and attended Episcopal services daily, twice if time permitted. The hectic schedule ceased in 1896, a year after The Breakers opened, when he suffered a stroke. He died three years later at the age of fifty-six.

Richard Hunt died in Newport on July 31, 1895, before The Breakers was completed. Toward the end of his life, he expressed the hope that he would be remembered best for the picturesque stick-style cottages he built early in his career before the huge commissions became available to him. Some excellent examples of these earlier houses stand on and near Bellevue Avenue, but it is with The Breakers and his other stone palaces that Hunt's fame rests.

The Countess Laszlo Szechenyi (nee Gladys Vanderbilt) leased The Breakers to The Preservation Society of Newport County for the token sum of $1.00 a year in order to raise funds for the restoration of the Hunter House. The popularity of The Breakers, America's greatest summer house, has been overwhelming. Over 4,000,000 Americans have visited this mansion which was finally acquired by the Society in 1972.

The east side, considered the most successfully designed facade of The Breakers, features the famous double loggia.

1. The Great Hall, rising 45 feet, the height of two full stories, provides a fitting entrance to the 70-room mansion.

2. The Breakers dining room, richly decorated with marble and gilded bronze, is by far the grandest in Newport.

1. Sunrise over Sakonnet Passage is seen from the east terrace of The Breakers.

2. The second-floor bedroom of Cornelius Vanderbilt contains the original custom-made carved walnut furniture.

3. The breakfast room at The Breakers was used by the Vanderbilts for informal meals and family dining.

3.

The most striking feature of the library is the great stone chimney piece, originally from a French chateau.

1. In the summer, the Italian Renaissance style lower loggia was filled with potted palms, allamandas and wicker furniture.

2. A morning view from the upper loggia.

2.

1. The fireplace in the music room is of blue Campan marble decorated with gilt bronze and semi-precious stones.

2. The music room, constructed in Europe and shipped to Newport for reassembly, was the scene of recitals and dances.

1. The billiard room, a pleasing blend of gray-green marble, yellow alabaster and red mahogany, was designed by Hunt.

2. An urn on the main terrace is framed by a carved bas-relief winged figure by the Austrian sculptor Karl Bitter.

The wrought iron gates, 30 feet high and topped with a C.V. monogram, form an imposing entrance to The Breakers.

Kingscote

Kingscote is one of the oldest summer cottages left standing in Newport, a reminder of the pre-Civil War days when wealthy Southern families continued the 18th century practice of spending their summers in the cool clime of the City-by-the-Sea. With its modest dimensions and gentle architecture, it is also a symbol of a less competitive time when houses were built more for comfort than for show.

The cottage, later to be called Kingscote, was built in 1839 for George Noble Jones, a well-to-do plantation owner from Savannah, Georgia. Accustomed to country living, George Jones chose his site, two acres at the corner of Bellevue Avenue and Bowery Street, accordingly. At that time, the area was mostly undeveloped farmland, selling for less than seven cents a foot. Bellevue Avenue, or South Touro Road, was little more than a dirt path. Situated on a high ridge overlooking Newport Harbor, the property was open to sea breezes from several directions — an important factor not only for summer comfort but for health.

It is difficult to imagine today the importance that Victorians attached to the powers of nature in preserving health. Long noted for its beauty, Newport, during the 19th century, gained a reputation for a particularly healthy climate. A *New York Times* writer went so far as to describe the atmosphere at the resort as "a kind of elixir vitae." Invalids were carried into the water at Easton's Beach daily for therapy amidst the seaweed, and even the frequent Newport fogs were considered beneficial. Noted Unitarian clergyman William Ellery Channing, a Newporter, related how "the fogs are proverbially a good cosmetic and there is a tradition that the fair daughters of Newport owed their lustrous complexions to sleeping with their heads out the window when the mists of the sea prevailed."

Having chosen his site, Mr. Jones asked architect Richard Upjohn to design his summer cottage. Upjohn, trained in England as a cabinetmaker before emigrating to America at age 26, was best known as a leading exponent of the Gothic Revival style. While his later reputation rested on his churches, including Trinity Church in New York, Upjohn's version of Gothic Revival, with its pointed gables and decorative woodwork, was well-suited to Victorian domestic tastes.

After some negotiating over details — Mr. Jones wanted a larger house than the architect first proposed — work on the cottage began in 1840 and was finished the following year. The result was a charming "Rustick Gothick" home, light in scale and irregular in shape. Nestled among trees and flowers, it was picturesque without the cloying quaintness of later Victorian "cots." Also, contrary to popular impressions of Victorian homes being dark and gloomy, Mr. Jones' house was light and airy, with a cream-colored exterior, numerous large windows, and an aviary, filled with large birds, over the front entrance.

George Jones moved into his summer home with his second wife, his widowed mother, and two unmarried sisters. He kept a cellar well-stocked with French wines and liked to entertain frequently, although on a much smaller scale than was to become fashionable later in Newport. Afternoon dinner and informal suppers were the rule, with large formal dinners being the exception. Horseback riding and swimming were popular pastimes. Bathing in this era took place at Easton's Beach, a mile-long crescent of sand to the east of town. Women and their escorts were permitted to use the beach mornings, under protection of a white flag. At noon, when a red bunting went up, women were expected to leave, presumably to be spared the sight of gentlemen in their bathing costumes, "sleeveless some and shirtless others," according to a 19th century chronicler. Both sexes enjoyed picnics and chowder parties on the rocks overlooking the sea and, in the evening, charades or amateur theatricals.

Mr. Jones and his extended family continued to enjoy summers at Newport throughout the 1850s, but

Kingscote, designed in 1839 by Richard Upjohn, for George Noble Jones, is one of the earliest of the Newport summer houses.

the atmosphere at the resort was gradually changing. In 1844, Ocean House, the first of the city's great hotels, went up on Bellevue Avenue across from the Jones property and began to attract steady summer visitors. Where once Mr. Jones had a single neighbor to the north, now houses were being constructed on all sides.

There were changes in the political climate as well. Newport, at one time a busy slave port, was becoming a hotbed of abolitionism, making things difficult for Southerners in general and slave owners like the Joneses in particular. When the Civil War broke out in the spring of 1861, Mr. Jones and his family left Newport and their summer home for good.

In their absence, the house was looked after by members of the King family, prominent local residents and friends of the Joneses. In 1863, the house was sold to William Henry King, a bachelor who had made a fortune in the China Trade. Renamed Kingscote (King's Cottage), the house would remain in the hands of the Kings and their family for more than a hundred years. When William King suffered a mental collapse in 1867, the house passed to his nephew, David King, also a former China Trade merchant. Much of Kingscote's present furnishing, including Townsend and Goddard pieces made in Newport and valuable Chinese objects, dates from the first two Kings.

The house underwent a number of changes during the tenure of David King and his wife, Ella Louisa Rives. The wooden siding was painted dark gray, the color it remains today, parquet floors were laid downstairs, and stained glass windows were installed in the entrance hall. The most important change came in 1881 after the Kings decided the house, despite an earlier addition, needed more space for family and staff and for entertaining on a scale expected of prominent summer residents.

The addition was designed by Stanford White of McKim, Mead and White, who was later to design Rosecliff. Instead of adding a wing to the house, which might have damaged its lines, he accomplished the enlargement by having the service wing moved about 30 feet to the northwest and sandwiching the addition in between. The new section consisted of a large dining room on the ground floor, which could be converted to a ballroom for entertaining, two bedrooms and a hallway on the second floor, and two nursery bedrooms and a bath on the third.

The dining room is a blend of standard and innovative materials and the most luxurious room in the house. The west wall is made almost entirely of opalescent brick tiles by Tiffany, arranged around a fireplace of Siena marble. The ceiling and upper walls, above the mahogany wainscoting, are covered with cork tiles, an innovation probably tried for its acoustical advantages.

Except for a red slate roof added in 1886, Kingscote has remained virtually unchanged to this day. David King died of peritonitis following an appendectomy in 1894, and the house was rented the next summer for use as the British "summer embassy," a common practice in the days before air conditioning. The following year, Mrs. King opened Kingscote for a coming-out party for her only daughter, Maud Gwendolen King.

Maud, who married Edward Maitland Armstrong in 1901, lived at Kingscote for more than fifty years, fighting some of the same encroachment that had oppressed George Jones almost a century before. Twice she was forced to go to court to save the house, once when an adjacent shopping center was intent on expansion. Mrs. Armstrong died in 1968, leaving Kingscote to her daughter, Gwendolen Armstrong Rives. When Mrs. Rives died in 1972, she left the house and its furnishings to The Preservation Society of Newport County. One year later, Kingscote was recognized by the National Register of Historic Places.

The mahogany-paneled dining room was added to Kingscote in 1882 from the designs of the architect Stanford White.

1.

1. The yellow Siena marble fireplace, on the west wall of the dining room, is highlighted by Tiffany glass bricks.

2. A Tiffany decanter and glasses, on a silver tray, stand before the opalescent Tiffany glass.

A detail of the movable black walnut screen and brass sconce at the east end of the dining room.

The Stanford White-designed colonial revival sideboard bears the distinctive Newport shell design.

The Elms

It is not surprising that The Elms is distinct from the other summer palaces in Newport. When Edward Julius Berwind chose an architect to build his new summer house on Bellevue Avenue, he did not, as might have been expected, turn to Richard Hunt, Stanford White, or another prominent New York or Newport designer. Instead he chose Horace Trumbauer, a young and relatively unknown architect from Philadelphia.

The two men, although of different generations, had much in common. Mr. Berwind was born in Philadelphia in 1848, the son of German immigrants. His father was a cabinet-maker of modest means. At the age of seventeen, the younger Berwind was appointed to the United States Naval Academy, then at Newport, and began a ten-year career as a Naval officer. After resigning his commission in 1875, he joined his brothers in the bituminous coal business, soon taking charge of the New York office. By the time The Elms was commissioned, the Berwind firm was the largest supplier of coal to the nation's merchant marine, the largest single owner of coal properties in the United States, and had branched out into such related fields as steamships, railroads, and docks.

Like Mr. Berwind, Trumbauer, born in 1868 of German parentage, was a self-made man. At sixteen, he joined Philadelphia's leading architectural firm as office-boy. Eight years later, he was in business on his own. Over the next seven years, before he received The Elms commission, Trumbauer designed three large residences in the Philadelphia area, including Grey Towers, at that time one of the largest houses in the country.

Unlike most of the architects working in Newport, however, Trumbauer lacked a Paris education and, in fact, had never traveled abroad. Nevertheless, working from existing plans and aided by skilled draftsmen, the designer in 1899 set about recreating an 18th century chateau that would inevitably be judged in comparison with the resort's other great cottages.

Mr. Berwind and his wife, the former Herminie Torrey, who was the daughter of the English consul to Italy, had been living in Newport since 1888 in a modest Victorian cottage on about one-third of an acre on Bellevue Avenue. In anticipation of building a much grander summer residence, Mr. Berwind enlarged his estate by about 14 acres.

In the spring of 1901, their new house nearing completion, the Berwinds went off on one of their frequent trips to Europe, leaving behind plans for a grand housewarming party upon their return. The house was ready on Aug. 30, and the celebration began, appropriately enough, with an 18th century cotillion danced by 125 couples and led by Mrs. Berwind.

The evening was a triumph for the Berwinds. Trumbauer had provided them with a remarkable adaptation of the Chateau d'Asnieres near Paris, from another design of the much-admired Jules Hardouin Mansart, chief architect at Versailles. Paris interior decorators Allard and Sons and Alavoine filled the house with enough period furniture, paintings, and tapestries to qualify The Elms as an instant museum, with the help of the great European art dealer Duveen. The park and formal garden surpassed most in landscape-conscious Newport. The total cost for the complete package, including land, was about $1.4 million — at a time when the average wage for skilled laborers was $3 a day.

The Elms housewarming was one of the last weekend entertainments of the summer. Guests were dropped from their carriages at one of three identical entrances, an unusual feature in Newport that the Berwinds had admired at Buckingham Palace and asked to have incorporated in their own house. In the pastel ballroom overlooking the flower-decked main terrace, Berger's Hungarian Orchestra took turns with Mullaly's Orchestra providing a continuous flow of dance music. Outside in the park, a brass band com-

The Elms, built in 1901 for Edward J. Berwind, is a successful adaptation of an 18th century French chateau.

peted with the chatter of a throng of pet monkeys scampering about the lawn. It was an extravagant occasion for the normally low-key Berwinds and, in all, more than 200 guests enjoyed the party — some said it was the best of the season.

A majority surely approved of the house as well. Although later architects may have found it a rather cool and detached, if faithful, rendition of an 18th century French chateau, The Elms was in keeping with the classical tastes of the time. The house is a model of classical symmetry — windows balance doors, paintings answer paintings, and mirrors are positioned opposite one another.

The house is also somewhat deceptive to the eye in the coy Mansart tradition. From the ground it appears to be two stories, rather horizontal in shape, with large sculpture groups on the parapet breaking the monotony of the roofline. Hidden behind the parapet is a third floor, containing the domestic staff's quarters — sixteen large rooms and three baths. In a similar manner, functional rooms, such as the kitchen and laundry, were kept out of sight in the basement. Mrs. Berwind kept in touch with her largely invisible staff by means of an elaborate call-box system operated from her second floor living quarters.

Equally elaborate was the heating system used to keep the house warm and protect the paintings and furnishings during the winter. Huge coal-fired boilers provided the heat. Mr. Berwind arranged for coal to be transported to his sub-basement by means of a small underground railroad that surfaced on Dixon Street to the south of the estate to avoid dust and dirt. Because electricity was not available in the neighborhood, he installed his own generator to power the house fixtures.

Grand in scale and richly-decorated as the house is, the most distinctive feature at The Elms has always been the grounds. Possibly to compensate for the lack of an ocean view, the Berwinds lavished extra attention outdoors, spending more than $300,000 on outbuildings and landscaping and employing a force of twelve gardeners to keep things in order.

Although the American elms for which the estate was named are gone, the 10-acre park contains almost 40 species of trees and a variety of shrubs and bushes, many of them manicured into trim cones and cylinders. Looking west from the main terrace, itself a formal affair with neat, ivy-lined paths and marble and bronze statue groups, the eye travels across the expanse of lawn to a row of clipped arborvitae and twin gazebos, or teahouses. Behind them lie the formal sunken gardens where beds of begonias rest between parterre scrolls of English boxwood. Here, hidden from view of the house, are more statues and fountains.

The Berwinds, who were childless, divided their time in Newport between The Elms and their steam yacht anchored in Newport Harbor. When Mrs. Berwind died in 1922, Mr. Berwind's unmarried sister, Julia, assumed the duties of hostess. In later years, her favorite pastime was a daily game of bridge in the conservatory. It has been said that her butler was included if there weren't sufficient friends available for a foursome.

Even in summer, Mr. Berwind restricted his stays in Newport to weekends, spending most of his time at his New York office. He continued to go to work daily until he was eighty-five, three years before his death in 1936. When Julia Berwind died in 1961 at the age of ninety-one, distant relatives sold the furnishings at auction and the estate to a real estate developer. The Elms was saved from certain destruction when The Preservation Society of Newport County raised enough money to buy it. Shortly afterward, the Society, through gifts and loans, managed to refurnish the house with appropriate furniture, some of it original, and The Elms was opened as a museum on Aug. 20, 1962.

The grand staircase of white marble, with an elaborate wrought iron and bronze railing, is in the 18th century French manner.

1.

2.

1. The cool and airy conservatory features a Rouge Royal marble fountain.

2. A tender sculpture group adorns the roof of The Elms.

3. This marble goddess graces one of the gardens at the Elms.

1. The K'ang Hsi lacquered panel is in the Chinese Breakfast Room.

2. The dining room at The Elms is in the Venetian style to complement the two large murals.

3. Twilight at The Elms.

The ballroom, in the Louis XV style, was the focal point for summer entertaining by the Berwinds.

An evening glow envelops one of the two gazebos marking the entrance to the sunken gardens at The Elms.

1. This is a copy of the Roman Renaissance Fontana delle Tartarugho (The Fountain of the Turtles) by Taddeo Landini

2. A Neptune and Thetis sculpture is on The Elms' roof.

3. From the upper terrace, the broad sweep of lawn leads to the sunken gardens beyond the gazebos.

The Berwind's private upstairs sitting room is decorated with English landscapes.

A sculpture group on the balustrade features frolicking cherubs and Capricorn.

1. The central feature of the upper terrace is the bronze statue, Le Furie di Atamente (The Madness of Athamas) cast in 1880 by Pio Fede.

2. Three arched doorways form the main entrance to The Elms.

3. The head of a bronze lion executed by Allard of Paris.

Chateau-sur-Mer

Chateau-sur-Mer is a tale of two houses in one. The first, completed in 1852, was a romantic villa in keeping with other summer cottages of the time in Newport, but larger and constructed of stone rather than the customary wood. The second, engineered by Richard Morris Hunt twenty years later, was an extension and transformation of the original house into a grand chateau that hinted of marble palaces to come.

Chateau-sur-Mer was built by Seth Bradford, a local contractor, for William Shepard Wetmore, who settled in Newport after making his fortune in the China Trade. From the start, it was apparent that Wetmore wanted something more than the ordinary Newport summer home.

The house was built of rough-cut Fall River granite that gave it a sense of rugged mass not seen before in seaside villas. Three stories tall, with a four-story tower over the entrance, Chateau-sur-Mer dominated the then-open spaces of Bellevue Avenue like a large and intricate rock outcropping.

Though smaller in scale than the later Chateau-sur-Mer in Newport, and almost diminutive compared to such behemoths as The Breakers, Bradford's house was substantial and expensive enough to have been called "almost palatial" by a commentator of the time. It was certainly a turning point in domestic architecture, and a gesture that signaled the beginning of the architectural competition among Newport's summer colonists that would keep designers and builders busy during the last decades of the 19th century.

Mr. Wetmore entertained on an impressive scale as well. In 1857, he gave a *fête champêtre* in honor of his long-time friend George Peabody of London that was attended by more than 3,000 guests from Europe and America. Canopied pavilions dotted the estate, and a 175-foot canvas-topped passage led from the house to a dancing platform. Guests danced from four to seven in the evening to the music of the Germania Musical Society, whose conductor, William Schultze, had composed a special "Fête Champêtre March" for the occasion.

The grounds, carefully landscaped with exotic trees, shrubs, and plants, were as much an attraction as the house. Although the view has since been obstructed, Chateau-sur-Mer (Castle on the Sea) at that time lived up to its name. Looking south from the 35-acre estate, guests could enjoy an ocean vista.

But the most talked about feature of the fete, reported in detail by the *New York Times,* was the sumptuous dinner served by George Downing, Newport's famous black chef. Among the menu offerings were woodcocks, plovers, and snipes, fried and pickled oysters, lobster and crab, various pâtés, and galantines of turkey, ham, and tongue. Dessert included ice creams, meringues, puddings, confections molded in the shapes of Washington and Lafayette, and dark Hamburg grapes from the Wetmore grapery. It was, according to one reporter present, "probably the greatest affair of its kind ever given in this country."

The party was an auspicious start for Chateau-sur-Mer, but it wasn't long before the early history of the house was eclipsed. William Wetmore died in 1862, and the estate passed to his only surviving son, George Peabody Wetmore. By all accounts a shrewd and ambitious man, the younger Wetmore devoted his energies toward building a law and political career in Rhode Island. He also undertook a major rebuilding program at the estate.

For the task, he chose Richard Morris Hunt, the Paris-trained architect noted at the time for his stick-

Chateau-sur-Mer, an imposing Victorian mansion, was the first of the great villas that came to line Bellevue Avenue.

style Victorian cottages. Working with stone for the first time on a domestic commission, Hunt, in two building campaigns, so altered the appearance of the chateau that later observers believed the original house to have been torn down. Even as astute an observer as Mrs. John King Van Rensselaer may have been deceived. Writing in 1905, she called Hunt's enlarged version "one of the largest and handsomest places on Bellevue Avenue" and commented that the original house "was supplanted many years since by Le Chateau-sur-Mer," although she may have been referring to an even earlier building that once stood on the site.

The misunderstanding was understandable. Hunt began his extensive and complicated revisions in 1871, with most of the work in the first phase being completed by the following year. On the exterior, working with the same Fall River granite, Hunt switched the main entrance from its tower location on the west over to the north, where he built a grand porte-cochere, or roofed carriage entrance. In a major change to the roofline, he replaced Bradford's gently-sloping gambrel roof with steeper mansard roofs.

Inside the house, in the northwest corner, Hunt tore out the old service wing to make space for a billiard room of almost one thousand square feet. He then added a wing on the northeast side to accomodate the service area and a new high-ceilinged dining room. With the new porte-cochere, Hunt felt the need for a dramatic entrance hall. Gutting a 20 by 30 foot area on the north side, he created a three-story hall with balconies and skylight. He then added an imperial staircase to complete the palatial effect.

Hunt's second building campaign several years later was a continuation of the first. At Mr. Wetmore's request for more space, he added another floor above the dining room and service wing. He also raised the mansard roofs to towering heights.

The result was a steep-roofed monolith of stone, more overpowering and massive than even Bradford's imposing structure. Critics have disagreed about Hunt's success — and that of the house — ever since, using such descriptions as "severe" and "stern." Almost a hundred years later, architectural historian Winslow Ames referred to its "battering ram quality", hardly the words normally associated with a summer dwelling.

In one respect, the rough appearance of the house was in keeping with the masculine atmosphere inside. Under the first two Wetmores, Chateau-sur-Mer was definitely a man's world, unlike other Newport cottages where the women ruled the roosts and the men occupied themselves with business and sports.

George Peabody Wetmore died in 1921 after serving two terms as Governor of Rhode Island and three terms in the United States Senate. After the estate passed into the hands of his two daughters, Edith and Maude Wetmore, the house began to show some softer touches. Before his death, at his wife's prodding, Mr. Wetmore had commissioned his cousin, Ogden Codman, Jr., a young Boston architect, to redo the southwest parlor in a more genteel Louis XV style that moved away from Hunt's favored Eastlake approach of honest (unretouched) construction. Over the years, the house gradually filled with Miss Edith Wetmore's collections of contemporary paintings and drawings and Chinese porcelain objects. In 1968, after the death of Edith Wetmore, a spinster as was her sister, the furnishings of the house were auctioned off. Many were acquired by The Preservation Society of Newport County, which also purchased the estate, preserving it for the public.

The French salon, designed by Ogden Codman, is delicate in contrast to the rugged interior design of the other rooms.

1.

2.

3.

1. Richard Morris Hunt added this new dramatic staircase and entrance hall in 1872 for George Peabody Wetmore.

2. From the porch of the original 1852 house, one sees some of the rare beech trees which grace these magnificent grounds.

3. The morning room shows the Eastlake style ash paneling favored by the architect Richard Morris Hunt.

The original entrance hall on the west side of Chateau-sur-Mer became the Marble Hall after Hunt's revisions of 1872.

The carved walnut overmantel in the dining room, by Luigi Frullini of Florence, features Bacchus with cherubs.

1.

2.

3.

1. A detail of the stone balustrade added to Chateau-sur-Mer by Hunt.

2. The dining room is decorated in a Victorian manner for the holidays.

3. The French-style ballroom at Chateau-sur-Mer is decorated each December for a Victorian Christmas.

1. The northwest bedroom is known as the Butternut Room after the light colored wood trim and furniture.

2. The library was decorated by Luigi Frullini of Florence.

The rugged brownstone forms a stark background for the delicate pink ornamental tree at the gate house.

Rosecliff

Every morning during the summer season, Theresa Fair Oelrichs, the daughter of a Belfast immigrant, rose promptly at eight to supervise the housecleaning at Rosecliff. Each room in the mansion had to be inspected, each bed made up fresh daily. Mrs. Oelrichs may have been a multimillionairess as well as one of the leading turn-of-the-century hostesses in Newport, but she lavished as much attention on the day-to-day workings of the household as she did on an important dinner or ball.

Her presence — and position — in Newport was the result of a classic union between money and family name. Her father, James Graham Fair, supplied the money. As a young Irish immigrant, Fair took part in the California Gold Rush of '49. Ten years later, following a thin vein of silver in Nevada, Fair and three partners struck the Comstock Lode, the single richest deposit of silver to be uncovered. Fair and his partners became instant millionaires, with the lode producing more than five hundred million dollars worth of silver over the next 20 years.

As one of two daughters of Fair, later a United States senator from Nevada, young Theresa Fair was able to mingle with East Coast society. On one of her trips East, either in Newport or New York, she met Hermann Oelrichs, the American agent for the North German Lloyd steamship line and a solid member of New York society. When they were married in 1890 in a spectacular San Francisco ceremony (at which the bride received a wedding gift of one million dollars from her father), the new Mrs. Oelrichs was assured of a position in society's inner circle.

One year later, preferring the social whirl of Newport to the quieter life in San Francisco, Mrs. Oelrichs, with her sister, Virginia Fair, bought the original Rosecliff along with 11 acres of land off Bellevue Avenue, just south of August Belmont's By-the-Sea. Although the estate afforded an excellent view of the ocean, it lacked Bellevue Avenue frontage, a deficit that caused Mrs. Oelrichs to postpone plans for a new and larger Rosecliff and to live for the time being in the old wooden cottage built by George Bancroft, a noted statesman and prominent amateur horticulturist whose fondness for roses gave the estate its name.

After arranging with a neighbor for access to Bellevue Avenue, the Oelrichs commissioned the architectural firm of McKim, Mead and White to design a new summer home which, like others of its kind, was intended primarily for grand-scale entertaining. The principal architect was Stanford White, designer of the Newport Casino, who responded by modeling the new Rosecliff after the Grand Trianon, the 17th century pleasure palace built at Versailles for Louis XIV of France.

Rosecliff, on which construction began in 1898, is a smaller, refined version of the sprawling 100-room Trianon. Eliminating from the French design all but the main block and two flanking wings — for an H-shaped structure — White kept many of the neoclassical exterior details, such as paired Ionic columns, arched French doors, and multi-tiered entablature topped with statues.

The exterior walls of Rosecliff are brick finished with near-white terra-cotta tiles that resemble stone. Rosecliff conveys an impression of light and air and delicate grace. More than the other mansions of Newport, White's creation epitomizes the lighter, more romantic side of the Gilded Age.

Once one is past the vestibule and stair hall, with its heart-shaped grand staircase, the focal point at Rosecliff is the ballroom, which occupies the entire central area of the ground floor. Measuring forty by eighty

Rosecliff, the most refined and classical of the Newport mansions, was modeled after the Grand Trianon at Versailles.

feet, it is the largest ballroom in Newport and the scene of the many lavish balls and dinners that helped Mrs. Oelrichs maintain her position, along with Mrs. Stuyvesant Fish and Mrs. O.H.P. Belmont, as one of the three great hostesses of the summer colony. So anxious was she to begin entertaining at her new home, that she moved in before work was completed, in early July of 1900. For a month she hurried the workmen along before expelling them to take sole possession. As a result, the house was not completely finished until 1902, and the grounds somewhat later.

Mrs. Oelrichs' enthusiasm for supervision, whether of maids or builders, later led to misfortune. One day, while calling out orders to some carpenters on scaffolding above her, she was struck by a falling tack and instantly blinded in one eye. She was not disfigured, however, and barely broke stride in helping direct the social life of the summer colonists.

She opened Rosecliff in late August of 1900 by giving a dinner for 112 guests prior to Mrs. Fish's Harvest Festival Ball at Crossways. Potted ferns and other florals from Hodgson, the Newport florist, camouflaged the unfinished condition of the house. But her best-remembered party was the Bal Blanc, or White Ball, which she gave on Aug. 19, 1904 to celebrate the Astor Cup race.

For this affair, Rosecliff was transformed into a world of white — white hydrangeas and hollyhock greeted guests in the vestibule; white roses, orchids, and lilies of the valley decorated the ballroom. Women guests were instructed to dress in white only and to powder their hair. Favors were white and silver. For contrast, all the men guests wore black.

Turned down in her request to borrow some of the Navy's "White Fleet" ships, Mrs. Oelrichs substituted a dozen full-sized artificial white ships that were anchored on the ocean behind Rosecliff to create the illusion of Newport Harbor transported to her estate.

The Rosecliff ballroom, with its trompe-l'oeil ceiling of painted clouds and its perfumed chandeliers, has been the scene of some fantasy balls as well. Parts of both *The Great Gatsby,* starring Robert Redford and Mia Farrow, and *The Betsy,* starring Laurence Olivier, Katherine Ross, and Robert Duvall, were filmed there in the 1970's, adding to Rosecliff's aura of romance.

Like many romantic settings, Rosecliff has seen its share of sadness. Despite her active social life, Mrs. Oelrichs was not a happy woman. Her husband, Hermann, spent most of his time traveling or in San Francisco, finally dying at sea in 1906. Mrs. Oelrichs' health began to fail in the 1920s, and thereafter she lived quietly at Rosecliff under the care of nurses.

After her death in 1926, her son Hermann Oelrichs Jr., spent several summers in Newport before putting Rosecliff up for sale in 1941. The house passed through several changes of ownership, sustaining severe water damage in the 1940s when the pipes burst. Ray Alan Van Clief bought Rosecliff in 1942 and began restoring it, handling all the arrangements from long distance by telephone. In 1945, the work completed, Mr. Van Clief directed that the house be made ready. Dinner was set for him and a car sent to Providence to pick him up. He never saw the results of his efforts, for on the road from Providence, he was killed when a fire truck struck his automobile.

His widow sold Rosecliff to Mr. and Mrs. J. Edgar Monroe of New Orleans the following year. They kept the house open summers for the next twenty-five years. In August of 1971, the Monroes donated the estate and its contents, along with a trust fund, to The Preservation Society of Newport County.

The Rosecliff ballroom, the largest in Newport, was the scene of many lavish balls given by Mrs. Hermann Oelrichs.

1. Flower urns dot the Cour d'amour (Court of Love), which was designed by Augustus St. Gaudens after one at Versailles.

2. The restored rose garden, for which the mansion was named, continues to be carefully maintained.

1. The dining room at Rosecliff, with its carved marble mantel, has matching bronze and crystal wall sconces and chandeliers.

2. A French Gothic style chimney piece of Caen stone dominates the salon, or reception room, at Rosecliff.

3. A morning view of the Atlantic Ocean can be seen from the balustrade at Rosecliff.

2.

3.

1.

2.

1. The famous heart-shaped staircase, which dominates the entrance hall, adds to Rosecliff's romantic aura.

2. Many statues and fountains adorn the grounds of Rosecliff.

3. Through the spray of a fountain, the grounds of Rosecliff afford a wide vista of the ocean .

Marble House

Of all the great summer cottages and palazzos of Newport, the Marble House is easily the most striking. Built of 500,000 cubic feet of cool white marble, fronted by four towering Corinthian columns modeled after — but larger than — those of the Temple of the Sun at Heliopolis, and overlooking a circular drive that sweeps up to the front entrance, Marble House virtually defines what a mansion should be. That is exactly what Mrs. William K. Vanderbilt would have wanted when her husband commissioned Richard Morris Hunt in 1888 to build them the finest summer house money could buy on Bellevue Avenue.

Born Alva Erskine Smith, the daughter of a cotton planter in Mobile, Alabama, the future Mrs. Vanderbilt was a remarkable dynamo of a woman whose social skills made her a leading hostess at Newport and in New York. As a young belle of twenty-two, Alva Smith met William K. Vanderbilt at the resort of White Sulphur Springs and agreed to marry him. "I was the first of my set to marry a Vanderbilt," she would say later. She was also instrumental in raising the Vanderbilts to full membership in the New York elite.

In 1888, the Vanderbilts decided to join the summer colony at Newport. In a city where the building of a new mansion was always the object of great curiosity, work on the Vanderbilt summer home began under conditions of extraordinary secrecy. Artisans, most of them from France and Italy, were quartered separately and not allowed to communicate on the job to help minimize the spread of rumors about Hunt's project. High fences prevented passersby and neighbors alike from watching the proceedings. It took nearly four years — and $11,000,000 — for Marble House to be completed. At last, on August 19, 1892, the Vanderbilts opened their house to their first guests.

Among those present was Richard Hunt, and there is reason to suppose a feeling of mutual satisfaction prevailed between architect and client. For Hunt, the Vanderbilt commission had given him an unparalleled opportunity to practice his Beaux-Arts skills, regardless of cost. Mr. Vanderbilt, in turn, was so pleased with Hunt's work that he placed his portrait in bas-relief on the wall of the upper hall, alongside that of Jules Hardouin Mansart, the master architect of Versailles.

The Vanderbilts had good reason to be pleased. Modeled after the Petit Trianon at Versailles, and reminiscent of both the White House and the Temple of Apollo, Hunt's creation was immediately recognized as a classical masterpiece, one that set the standard for similar efforts during the American Renaissance. Everything in the house was done on a grand scale, from the elaborate bronzed entrance grille, weighing more than ten tons, to the Gold Ballroom. Not the largest but certainly the most ornate of any in Newport, the room has carved gilt wall panels by Karl Bitter, a huge ceiling painting in the manner of Tintoretto, and a mantlepiece of Fleur-de-Peche marble topped by bronze sculptures.

The sculptures, and many other pieces in the house, were crafted by J. Allard & Son, the fashionable Paris decorators who created the interiors for many of the Newport mansions. Allard, along with the Paris firm of Henri Dasson, also custom-made most of the furniture for Marble House, predominantly Louis XIV and Louis XV period pieces in keeping with both Hunt's and the Vanderbilts' tastes.

Marble, of course, is in evidence throughout the house. The yellow Siena marble from Italy that covers the floor and walls of the entrance hall leads to the pink Numidian marble that lines the formal dining room. It is difficult to imagine anyone living in this vast expanse of marble punctuated by such lush ornamentation. The ground floor rooms were generally reserved for

Marble House, built in four years for William K. Vanderbilt, is perhaps the greatest neo-classical house in America.

large-scale entertainments. For day-to-day visiting, Mrs. Vanderbilt used her mezzanine-level sitting room, across the landing from her husband's study.

Mr. Vanderbilt, who turned ownership of the house over to his wife upon its completion, spent only two summers at Marble House. In March of 1895, his wife became the first of her set to divorce a Vanderbilt. From then on, William Vanderbilt spent most of his time on his yacht or in New York. After remarrying in 1903, he moved to Paris where he died in 1920.

Alva Vanderbilt set out to solidify her social position by marrying off her 18 year old daughter, Consuelo, to a member of the English peerage. On August 28, 1895, five months after her divorce, Mrs. Vanderbilt held a great ball to introduce her daughter to society. Through no coincidence, the ninth Duke of Marlborough was staying as a guest at Marble House at the time.

More than 500 guests attended Consuelo Vanderbilt's coming-out party. Footmen dressed in Louis XIV fashion led them into the main hall, which was dominated by a spectacular floral piece, consisting of a large bronze fountain filled with floating lotus, water hyacinths, and fairy lamps. Fluttering about the blossoms were live hummingbirds and brightly-colored butterflies, all courtesy of Hodgson, Newport's society florist. Guests danced to three orchestras in the Gold Room, while nine French chefs prepared the dinner. One course alone consisted of 400 mixed birds.

The evening produced the desired effect — at least for Mrs. Vanderbilt. The Duke proposed to the debutante in the Gothic Room, she dutifully accepted at her mother's insistence, and the two were married the following November in New York. After a long separation, Consuelo divorced her husband in 1921 to marry again, this time for love. In 1896, Alva

Vanderbilt married Oliver Hazard Perry Belmont, son of the August Belmonts, and moved across Bellevue Avenue to Belcourt. Marble house was closed for 12 years, but was reopened in 1908 after the death of Mr. Belmont. Entertainment resumed, but with a different twist.

At some point, Mrs. Belmont had become a dedicated suffragist. On August 24, 1909, she opened Marble House to the public for the first time to raise money for the women's suffrage movement. Five years later she presided over an international convention of suffragettes, where she personally reassured a faltering young activist who had recently been arrested. "Brace up, my dear," she reportedly said, "Pray to God. *She* will help you."

Soon after, Mrs. Belmont moved to France, where she was busy restoring an old chateau near Fontainebleau when she died in 1933 at the age of eighty. She was buried in Woodlawn Cemetery in New York in a mausoleum of her own design. Mrs. Belmont had caused so many structures to be built during her lifetime, including the Chinese Tea House on her estate at Newport, that she was invited to join the American Institute of Architects. She declined.

She sold Marble House shortly before her death to Frederick H. Prince of Boston, a yachtsman and president of Armour and Co. The house remained in the Prince family until purchased from the Frederick H. Prince Trust in 1963 by The Preservation Society of Newport County. Money for the purchase came from Harold S. Vanderbilt, who defended the America's Cup three times. He was the youngest of William and Alva Vanderbilt's three children. The furnishings were donated to the Society by the Frederick H. Prince Trust.

The ballroom, or Gold Room, at Marble House is certainly the most opulently ornamented in Newport.

The floor and walls of the entrance hall at Marble House are lined with yellow Siena marble from Italy.

One of a pair of sconces which was made by J. Allard et fils, the great Paris firm which designed many Newport interiors.

1. The pink Numidian marble and gilt bronze ornamentation convey a sense of opulence and grandeur in the dining room.

2. The four corners of the dining room are decorated with gilt stag heads on ormolu plaques.

The Gothic Room was used to house Mr. Vanderbilt's collection of rare Gothic miniatures and objets d'art.

Mrs. Vanderbilt's peach-colored bedroom is decorated in the elaborate Rococo Revival style.

1. A detail of the fireplace in the Gold Room by J. Allard et fils features Youth and Old Age holding candelabras.

2. The entrance grille of steel and gilt bronze, one of the most distinctive features of Marble House, weighs more than ten tons.

Hunter House

The Hunter House on Washington Street is neither the oldest nor the largest colonial dwelling in Newport. With its clean lines, pleasant proportions, and surprisingly ornate interior, it is as fine an example of mid-18th century architecture as one could hope to visit. Inhabited by a succession of prosperous merchants, two governors and an ambassador, as well as the commander of the French naval forces during the Revolution, Hunter House is a microcosm of Newport's turbulent colonial and post-colonial history.

More properly called the Nichols-Wanton-Hunter House, the house had its beginnings in 1748 when Jonathan Nichols bought two lots on Easton's Point from James Sheffield, together with all "buildings and edifices thereon." Although it is possible that Sheffield built the first part of the house, it is more likely that the structures mentioned in the deed referred to a warehouse, wharf, and various out-buildings, and that Nichols started the house some time after 1748. By 1758, according to a detailed map of the city drawn by the Rev. Ezra Stiles, a one-chimney dwelling stood on the property.

As a merchant heavily engaged in sea trade, it was logical for Nichols to live on the Point. A quiet, rural area until 1711, when Quaker families began taking up residence, the Point, at the north end of the harbor, rapidly became the focal point of Newport's busy marine trade. By the mid-1700s, Newport was one of the leading ports of colonial America, with more than 500 ships involved in coastal and foreign trade, including the infamous Triangle Trade, which involved the shipping of molasses, rum, and slaves between the West Indies, Newport, and the west coast of Africa.

Like many of his neighbors along Water (now Washington) Street, Nichols owned several ships, including at least one privateer. He also owned a number of slaves. Besides his far-flung business enterprises, Nichols was active in politics, as was his father, serving as a colonial deputy before being elected deputy governor in 1753, a post he held until his death three years later at the relatively young age of forty-four.

Upon his death, the property, including a "mansion house" along with the other buildings, was put out to bid and sold in 1757 to Col. Joseph Wanton, Jr., the son of a prominent Newport merchant. It was Wanton who added the south portion of the house and a second chimney, giving it much the appearance it has today.

Born in 1730, Wanton, like Nichols before him, was active in both the sea trade and politics. Working for his father's firm of Joseph and William Wanton Co., the younger Wanton engaged in the popular mercantile pursuits of privateering and slave trading, as well as the growing business of dealing in spermaceti candles. Water Street at this time was a crowded row of wharves, warehouses, and ropewalks, and it is probable that Wanton continued the practice of using his house as an office as well as a home. During this period, while the activity was on the waterfront, the front of the house was considered to be the west side, facing the harbor.

As completed by Wanton, the house was a two-and-one-half story dwelling typical of its period, with a simple floor plan of four rooms per level, two on either side of a wide hallway. The walls were studded, filled with bricks for insulation, then plastered over in the English half-timbered fashion. The outer layer consists of horizontal sheaths of oak, left unpainted for years before receiving a coat of off-white paint. There is no architect on record for either Nichols or Wanton for the simple reason that houses were designed along traditional lines and builders considered themselves primarily carpenters.

The house is notable for its interior woodwork — six of the rooms have floor-to-ceiling pine wainscoting. The paneling in the northeast parlor is especially fine and is set off by Corinthian pilasters, painted in Wanton's time to resemble marble, in this case black marble veined with gold. Four cherub heads over built-in cupboards flanking the fireplace were polychromed then as they are now.

There is evidence Wanton installed paneling taken from other houses, which was "grained" in various shades so that the paint simulated the grains of finer hardwoods. It is likely as well that the intricately-carved mahogany staircase that rises from the hall through three stories was taken from another house, possibly the Malbone estate which burned in 1766.

The Hunter House, with its rich history, is considered one of the foremost examples of American colonial architecture.

Wanton furnished his house with many fine pieces from the local cabinet-making families of Townsend and Goddard, whose shops were nearby on the Point. Although most of the original furnishings are gone, the house has been refurnished with authentic Queen Anne, Chippendale, and Hepplewhite pieces made by the Townsends and Goddards and other Rhode Island craftsmen.

Elected to the General Assembly in 1756, the year before he bought the house, Wanton rose to the position of deputy governor. For a time, with Wanton Sr. serving as governor of the colony, the family was powerful both in political and business circles. But they were confirmed loyalists at a time when sentiment was growing stronger in favor of independence for the colonies, and as the Whigs grew in influence, the Wantons and other Tories waned.

The Wantons survived the first upheavals of the coming revolution, while other Tories were being run from town, but in 1774 the younger Wanton lost his seat in the Assembly and a year later his father was ousted as governor. Wanton was arrested at his home on Christmas Day, 1775, released, but arrested again a year later and exiled to his farm on Jamestown. With the arrival of British troops late in 1776, Wanton was back in Newport for the duration of the three-year occupation, eventually serving as superintendent of the colonial police for Aquidneck Island.

By now his fate was tied to that of the hated occupiers, and when the British withdrew from Newport in 1779, Wanton and a small band of loyalists were forced to go with them. By the end of the war, both father and son had died in exile. Whatever misfortunes Wanton's politics had brought him, his Tory sympathies very likely were responsible for his house being saved while others on the Point, and throughout Newport, were destroyed by marauding British and Hessian troops.

When the French allies entered Newport in the summer of 1780, they found a depressed population in a largely ruined town. By Ezra Stiles' count, more than 300 dwellings had been torn down for firewood during the occupation, along with most of the orchards. Two-thirds of the residents had fled the island. Wanton's house, confiscated by the colony as soon as the British departed, was in relatively good condition and was turned over to Admiral de Ternay, commander of the French fleet, for his use. De Ternay died of a fever in the house on Dec. 15, 1780, but the French continued to use it as a lodging and headquarters until the next year, when the fleet left Newport for Yorktown.

For years after the war, the house on Washington Street, like most of Newport, deteriorated. "Since the peace, everything is changed," a French visitor wrote in 1788. "The reign of solitude is only interrupted by groups of idle men standing, with folded arms, at the corners of the streets; houses falling to ruin — miserable shops." Wanton's house changed hands several times until, in 1805, it got a long-term owner in William Hunter, who purchased it for $5,000, a fraction of its former value.

Born in 1774, the son of a well-known Scottish surgeon, Hunter was trained as a lawyer and, like his predecessors in the house, was active politically. Hunter's political career took him from the General Assembly to the United States Senate and, finally, to Brazil, where he served as ambassador for ten years between 1834-44. Although his name became associated with the house, he contributed few, if any, major changes to it during his 44 years of ownership, other than landscaping the yard with rose and berry bushes and quince trees.

Two years after Hunter's death in 1849, his widow sold the house to a corporation and there began another chain of owners, many of whom operated it as a boarding house. Except for numerous coats of paint inside and out and several damaging alterations during the 1870s when the entrances were widened, the doors removed, and a back porch added, the Hunter House remained much as it was during Wanton's tenure. In 1945, when the Metropolitan Museum of Art in New York sought to buy the house and remove its paneling, Hunter House was purchased by a private group and transferred to the newly-created Preservation Society of Newport County. After several years of painstaking research and restoration, the house was opened to the public.

The doorway at Hunter House is adorned with a carved wooden pineapple, Newport's traditional symbol of hospitality.

1.

2.